EVER OPEN DOOR

EVER OPEN DOOR

The Story of Dr. Barnardo

by

CAROLYN SCOTT

LUTTERWORTH PRESS

GUILDFORD AND LONDON

ISBN 0 7188 1903 9

PRINTED PHOTOLITHO IN GREAT BRITAIN
BY EBENEZER BAYLIS AND SON, LTD.
THE TRINITY PRESS, WORCESTER, AND LONDON

CONTENTS

1

A GROUP of ragged boys sat in a dirty back alley and pooled their money. They had twopence. And twopence was not even enough to pay for a bed for the night.

John had earned a halfpenny by selling a fat cigar-end to a man who wanted to look rich.

Tim had earned twopence by soaking himself to the skin to find a couple of lumps of coal on the river bed, but his mother had taken the twopence and kicked him out of doors.

George had made three-halfpence selling flowers outside the cinema. Harry had been out begging, but he was so tired that he had fallen asleep and no one had noticed him. Mick smelled terrible after scouring the sewers for food.

"We gotta get some money," said John. So four of the quickest slipped out silently along the shadowy walls of the slums, like cats on the prowl.

The yellow light of a policeman's lantern swung into sight. He heard the scuffling in a doorway and swung his lantern in the opposite direction.

He was kind-hearted, and he knew that if he found boys out at night with nowhere to go, he would have to take them into custody. A rat sat and blinked in the sudden brilliance, and then bolted down the street and away towards the docks.

The yellow light faded and the slow, plodding footsteps died away. The dark, dirty doorways of the broken-down buildings sank back into a dingy, scuffling silence, and the four shadows flitted along against the wall.

"Look!" John's eyes were sharper than the rest. The boys flattened themselves against the wall and waited. A small, brisk figure strode past.

It was a young man with spectacles, a moustache, and side-whiskers. He was wearing a top hat and frock coat, with a watch-chain glinting across his chest. The boys took in a breath. Their luck was in.

Like four wild animals they leaped out of the shadows and sprang on top of the little man, and his glasses were knocked from his face.

"Quick! Get 'is money, Tim!" muttered John, and Tim's quick fingers flew in and out of pockets and he was away down the street and out of sight.

Two minutes later, the young man was left flat on his back in the middle of the street. One boy had fled with his watch and chain. Another with his hat, and the third with his heavy top coat.

He sighed, picked himself up and brushed his trousers. The mud on them would have to be washed out. Short-sightedly he searched around for his spectacles and found them at last in a pool of mud and slops tipped from one of the windows above, where families lived ten to a room with no furniture.

"Now who, I wonder, were they?" he asked himself, shaking his head. And holding his scarf tightly round his neck, because it was cold without a coat, he hurried on his way. He had several calls to make, and now he would be late.

Before he had gone very far, he heard footsteps pounding along the cobbled road behind him.

"Sir!" Anxious voices called out to him. "Sir! Stop, sir, please!"

He stopped and turned round. They were running after him, the coat trailing on the ground and tripping them up, no longer four animals, but four hungry, ragged, breathless little boys.

"Well, what is it?" he asked them, smiling a little.

"Please, sir," said John, gulping for breath, "We're sorry, sir. We'd never 'ave done it . . ." He handed the hat back, and the coat, the money and the watch and chain.

"We'd never 'ave done it, sir, if we'd known it was you."

Then while Doctor Barnardo finished his visiting they fetched their friends, and accompanied him back to his home in a high stone house where Stepney Causeway led down to the Thameside docks, and he gave them hot soup and bread and buns, and a warm, clean bed for the night.

2

ODD BOY OUT

THOMAS Barnardo grew up in Dublin. His parents believed in God and went to church twice every Sunday. Thomas didn't believe in anything.

He was always the odd boy out. He was very short and he hated playing games. He didn't like school, and he spent all the time in class talking. When his brother was given chocolates for singing to guests in the drawing-room, Thomas flew at him and called him names. He cared for no one but himself.

"I've never met a boy less likely to do anything for anyone," said one of his friends.

Thomas was often unwell and because his eyes were weak, he had to wear blue-tinted spectacles. He wasn't at all good-looking, and when he left school and college and joined his father's fur-trading business, he was a difficult, annoying, rather rude young man of sixteen, very plain to look at.

"I'll go with you if you want," he said one

evening to his two brothers, Fred and George, as they put on their best clothes and set off to a religious meeting to be held in a friend's house. "But I think you're all mad."

Religious meetings were being held all over the country. It was 1862; times were hard and it wasn't easy to believe in God. The rich living in the towns with their carriages and coaches, their footmen and grooms, felt comfortable and contented. The poor lived off potatoes, and because for years now the potato crops had failed, hundreds starved to death every year.

The rich felt no need for God, and the poor were too busy trying to keep alive. But there were a few people who were absolutely convinced that if people would only remember God and try to do his will, the rich would be jolted into doing something about the poor, and the poor would learn that whatever happened, Jesus cared for them.

The Barnardos had been both rich and a little poor, because Thomas's father was not a very good business man. The children had been brought up to read the Bible and go to church. Now they all threw themselves into one religious meeting after another with tremendous excitement and enthusiasm.

All except Thomas.

He argued and twisted and turned. He disliked squashing into crowded halls between farm labourers whose muddy clothes made dirty marks on his clean white cuffs. He was very rude to his father's religious friends, and when they refused to be cross with him, he felt more angry and lost and muddled than ever. He wanted them to be cross with him. Then he could dismiss them and forget what they said about God. But they were so nice.

He walked moodily behind his brothers as they made their way to the house where the meeting was to be held. In spite of his dull looks, he liked to be laughing and talking and having fun. He looked very fashionable, with a silk hat and smart gloves and a walking stick. Since leaving school, he had always dressed as well as he could, to make up for being short and ordinary.

A religious meeting seemed to him to be a terrible waste of time. "I don't care," he muttered sullenly as they arrived. "I shan't listen. You can't prove that God exists and the sooner we get home and get on with something else, the better."

But the meeting lasted a long time.

A lot of people spoke. Prayers were said and hymns were sung. One by one people jumped up from the seats ranged round the room, and added their comments, their own personal little glimpses of God. But Thomas really saw and heard only one man. He was a famous actor, and he had given up acting to become a preacher. He had been drunk and rude and bad, until he had suddenly realized that God loved him and Jesus had died for him. Now he seemed the happiest man on earth.

Thomas didn't say a word all the way home. His face was white and his mouth was set. He looked as if he'd burst into tears if he tried to speak. By the time they reached home, he was crying.

He had realized that when you know a thing beyond all shadow of doubt, you no longer need proof. And he knew that God loved him.

*　　*　　*

But what could he do?

He started taking Sunday morning Bible classes at one of the schools for poor boys in Dublin, and the boys were so naughty that he had to leave his walking stick behind in case he gave in to the temptation to hit them.

He took his courage in both hands and began preaching to the soldiers and the police and found to his astonishment that they were willing to listen.

He went out night after night to the most dangerous and dirty areas of the Dublin slums with Bibles and packets of tea and began making friends with the people living among the bugs and the mice and the rats in tumbledown shacks, "Where I wouldn't even kennel a dog;" he said, "and yet these are the children of God."

He began to find that in spite of his unattractive looks, he had a way with people. When he spoke to them, they couldn't help listening. He told them about the love of God, and then when he left them, he wondered how they could think of anything but hunger when they felt sick with it day after day.

He was only sixteen. What could he possibly do for a world which seemed to be full of unhappiness?

3

TURNING THE TABLES

"HAVE you seen that new boy, Barnardo?" asked one of the medical students, at the height of the cholera epidemic in London. "He's out in the streets with people dying like flies—and he's *preaching*!"

He wasn't only preaching.

Day after day he tramped from door to door throughout the East End of London kneeling beside people as they died on filthy stone floors. He climbed rotten staircases and ferreted into attic rooms. He found children huddled together in tiny holes made by boarding a corridor across, and he heard them call the few square feet of rags and bones "home". At night he went back to his lodgings and tried to strip the fleas out of his clothes and longed to be able to do something to help the poor.

He had come to London to learn to be a doctor. Then he was to go out to China as a missionary. But when an Asiatic seaman brought cholera to the East End docks in 1866, when Barnardo was just twenty-one, he began to see that China wasn't the only place in the world in need of missionaries. When he looked around, he saw that there was more than he could cope with right where he was.

"You are the children of God," he shouted at the street corners to the poor people in their dirty rags, struggling to keep alive. And in return, the children of God pelted him with tomatoes and eggs and any old rubbish that came to hand. But some of them listened. And some of them understood.

"Don't go in, sir," pleaded a publican as Barnardo arrived at the door of a beerhouse one night with his packets of Bibles tucked under his arm. "Don't go in, sir—you'll be sorry if you do."

"Don't be silly!" Barnardo was small, but he was tough and he wasn't a coward. If he was frightened, he never showed it. "I'll be all right. Here—" he wagged a Bible in the face of the astonished landlord, "If you knew what it says here, you wouldn't be frightened either. Read that."

The publican couldn't read very well, and Barnardo helped him out. "It says," he explained, "that the joy of the Lord shall be your strength."

The man still looked doubtful. "I dunno, sir," he said, shaking his head. "Whatever that means, I wouldn't do it if I was you. And don't you hold me responsible for what happens!" he shouted after Barnardo as the young medical student pushed open the door.

As soon as Barnardo was inside the beerhouse bar, the door slammed shut behind him. Two tough boys leaned with their backs against it, looking at him. There was no going back.

Barnardo blinked. The room was filled with smoke, making it difficult to see. There were boys and girls lying on the benches round the central table. They seemed very young—thirteen or fourteen years old. The oldest boy could only have been eighteen.

"I'd like to talk to you for a moment," he began, shouting a little so that they could all hear. "I've come to sell you the word of God." He started laying out the Bibles and New Testaments on the table. "The Bibles are threepence a copy, New Testaments are only . . ."

"Come on, mister!" shouted a girl sprawling on her back in a corner. "Leave us the books and get out."

Barnardo eyed her sternly. "They cost me twice as much as I'm asking for them," he said firmly. Then he climbed on top of the table and began to talk about God.

Before he knew where he was, the table was turned upside down. He was lying flat on his back on the floor with the table on top of him, its legs sticking up in the air, while boys and girls danced a war dance on top of it. He felt as if his chest would burst.

Bibles flew in all directions and bottles of beer crashed on to the floor and broke.

"Hear the word of God!" they chanted. "Tell us the word of God now, mister!" Barnardo winced with pain and opened his mouth, but he was too breathless, and no words came.

Eventually the fun wore off. A couple of boys went out into the streets, and the rest wandered back to the benches to drink some more and to sleep. One or two were scared. The young man on the floor looked dishevelled and hurt.

"Let's get out!" they said, and ran off.

Painfully Barnardo crawled out and picked himself up. He felt as if every bone in his body was broken. He left the Bibles behind in the dust and the dirt and the puddles from broken beer bottles, and walked slowly home.

"Let me come with you," offered the publican. But Barnardo shook his head. "No, no. You're very kind, but I'm all right," he said, half smiling. "It's all part of being a fool for God—you get used to it."

And the publican hadn't the heart to say, "I told you so."

The walk home was painful. Every step jarred

his bruises, and all the time, Barnardo found he couldn't forget the boys and girls he had left behind, with their hard eyes and their pinched, pale faces.

At last he reached his lodgings. "Where on earth have you been this time?" asked his friends, exasperated. He was so hard to understand. They never knew what he was thinking, or what he would do next. Gay and joking one moment, he would suddenly be gone for the evening, to return covered with mud and bad fruit, tired, dirty and stupidly happy, making the place smell like a sewer.

They helped him gently into a chair and took off his jacket.

"Careful . . ." he winced as one of them unbuttoned his shirt.

"But what happened?" they persisted.

"It was—" he hesitated, searching for the word. "It was—a discussion."

"Some discussion," they agreed. "You've two ribs broken and a mass of bruises. Some discussion!"

Barnardo nodded. He was tired and he wanted to go to bed. And he felt sad. He had seen the looks on the faces of the boys and girls as he left the bar. Some of them were already sleeping noisily, quite drunk with beer, but the others followed him with their eyes. And what he had seen in their eyes troubled him. More than anything else, he wished he could help them, because he knew that in spite of all their defiance, they wanted help.

His friends finished bandaging him and he gingerly eased himself out of the chair. As they helped him towards the stairs, there was a loud banging on the door.

"I hope you don't mind, sir—I followed you here from the beerhouse just now." The policeman was tall, his cape filling the doorway. "You'll be wanting to prosecute. Just give me the full details and I'll have the offenders in prison for what they did to you."

"Prison?" Barnardo echoed the word as if he had never heard it before. "But I don't think prison would do any good at all." He shook his head. "Thank you, officer, but I shan't be bringing a prosecution."

"If you'll take my advice, sir, you will," said the policeman, forgetting his manners in his astonishment. "They could have killed you, sir. And they're all bad. They'll be in gaol for stealing or loitering or worse before the week's out. There's nothing you nor I can do about that."

"Isn't there?" Barnardo hesitated. "Perhaps you're right. But I began by preaching a gospel of love, and I'm going to carry on preaching it. The gospel advises visiting people in prison, but it says nothing about putting them there to be visited."

The policeman looked at the other students, but they shrugged their shoulders. And he went away.

"He won't prosecute!" he said to his colleague at the gate. "He's a fool—he won't prosecute." They walked disconsolately away.

"He won't prosecute!" The news spread like wild-fire through the back alleys of London's East End. "Have you heard? Barnardo won't prosecute!"

The next day there was another knock at the door. A group of subdued children stood on the step.

"Please," they asked nervously, "is Mr. Barnardo all right?"

"He will be in a few weeks. He's in bed at the moment, and lucky to be alive at all," one of the students told them. "Why?"

They shuffled uneasily. "We—we just wanted to know." They turned to go. Then hesitated.

"Yes?"

"Would you give 'im a message? Would you tell 'im 'e'll never come to no 'arm in Stepney again, sir? Tell 'im we'll see to that."

The boys and girls who had beaten up Thomas Barnardo when he tried to talk to them about the love of God had never seen the love of God in action before. Now they had. And they liked it.

4

"PLEASE LET ME STAY, SIR!"

THEY liked it so much that when he opened his own part-time school for poor children, hundreds of them streamed through the doors. It was only an old disused donkey shed with the timbered roof painted white and rough wooden boards covering the dirty cobble-stone floor. But all the ragamuffins for miles around came in out of the cold to learn the alphabet and to hear the wonderful adventures Barnardo told so excitingly out of a big book they had never heard of before— a book called the Bible.

At first they had thrown eggs at him and smoked out the schoolroom with cayenne pepper stink bombs. Now he couldn't keep them away. Two nights a week and all day Sunday, ragged children from all over the East End crowded into the make-shift school on the corner of a street named Hope Place.

One of the boys was called Jim Jarvis.

"Come on, Jim!" said Barnardo late one evening. He had collected his books together and was about to lock up and go home when he saw Jim, still sitting hunched up in the shadows by the fireside. "It's time to go home. All your friends have gone."

"I know." Jim continued to sit there on his wooden box seat, his hands round his knees. "I don't want to go, sir."

"But it's long past bed-time." Barnardo pulled his watch out of his waistcoat pocket and looked at it. "You'll miss your meal if you don't hurry . . ."

"Please let me stay, sir," butted in Jim, miserably staring at his hands.

"But I've got to lock up and go home." Barnardo couldn't understand what the matter was. All the other children had raced off home long ago. "Your mother will be worrying about you."

"I ain't got no mother."

"Well, your father then—or isn't he home yet?"

"I ain't got no father."

"Well who do you live with?"

Jim wriggled and hunched his shoulders closer together. "No one."

Barnardo paused and looked more closely at the miserable figure crouching over the flames. For the first time he realized just how thin Jim was. His shoulder blades stuck out and his face looked pinched and hungry. His clothes were in rags: an old torn pair of trousers and a thin cotton shirt with one sleeve torn out and no buttons. It was winter, cold and wet with a wind blowing.

"How old are you, Jim?" he asked, more gently.

"Ten, sir." For the first time since the conversation began, Jim looked up at the young schoolmaster standing over him.

"And where do you live?"

Jim shrugged and looked away again. "Nowhere really, sir. Or anywhere, I s'pose." He hesitated. "If I could've stayed here, sir—just tonight. It's so warm and the police wouldn't find me."

Barnardo still couldn't fully understand. "But— where do you usually sleep?"

"Anywhere." Jim wriggled nearer the fire and looked up at Barnardo again. "Sometimes they puts tarpaulins over the roofs, and we sleep in the gutters underneath. It's warmer underneath. Then there's boxes and barrels in the markets—the police don't see you there."

"What happens if the police do see you?"

"They puts you in prison of course, sir!" Jim was surprised at his master's ignorance. "They put me inside once, but I'm better at 'iding now. I gotta good place last night, down in Whitechapel 'aymarket in one of them carts. It was soft an' all."

Barnardo shook his head. He thought he knew all there was to know about the life of the poor in London. He thought he had been doing so much in

opening a school and runing it at the same time as
he carried on with his medical studies. Now
suddenly a little destitute boy was showing him a
whole new world.

"Are you sure you're telling me the truth, Jim?"
He still couldn't entirely believe it.

"Of course I am." Jim couldn't understand his
surprise. "Why?"

"Are there other boys like you?"

Jim hooted with laughter. "There's thousands of
us, sir! Some of 'em kicked out, some of 'em run
away, and then there's us wot ain't got no 'ome
anyway. You work a bit and you pinch a bit and if
you're lucky you keep clear of the police. But this
place . . ." He looked around at the white-washed
schoolroom. "Well honest, sir, this place is just
like 'eaven."

Barnardo swung his cloak round his shoulders
and picked up his hat and cane. "If I give you a
meal and a bed for the night," he said, holding out
his hand to Jim, "will you take me with you and
show me where the other boys sleep?"

Would he? Jim jumped up in a flash, and they
went off together, hand in hand.

They looked an odd couple, sitting opposite each
other across the table at Barnardo's lodgings. Jim
gobbled his food in no time, as if he hadn't eaten a
good meal for months. After his third steaming

mug of hot, sweet coffee, a faint warmth crept into his cheeks.

"Have you ever heard of Jesus, Jim?" asked Barnardo, suddenly and quite unexpectedly.

"Jesus? No, sir." Jim looked interested. "What's that?"

"Jesus was a bit like you," Barnardo went on. "He was born on a bed of hay in a stable with no home, and it was cold, just like it is now, wintertime, with the wind whistling round the door."

"Poor fella," said Jim, understandingly. "But it's a funny name, sir, Jesus."

"Jesus was the Son of God," explained Barnardo. "God wanted people like you and me to know how much He loves us, so He sent His Son to be just like us."

Jim pulled his chair up close to the fire and sat gazing into the flames. "But God don't care about me. There ain't nobody does."

"Yes He does, Jim," said Barnardo seriously. "And Jesus loved you so much that He died for you." And as they sat by the fire together, he told Jim all about Jesus. Then they went out together, firm friends, to see for themselves the truth of Jim's story.

It was a dark night, with drifting clouds blotting out the light of the moon. Barnardo's lantern cast shadows across the cobbled streets and picked out a stray cat here and there. He looked down at the little boy trotting along beside him, tugging him by the hand through alley-ways and smelly passages, past the late-night beerhouses and gaudy gin-palaces until at last they reached the clutter of shops where the marketeers sold and bartered in Petticoat Lane.

"We've come a long way, Jim," said Barnardo sternly, a little out of breath. "If you've brought me on a wild goose chase, I shall be very cross with you."

"We're here, sir!" said Jim, triumphantly.

Barnardo looked around. All was very quiet and still, without a sign of anyone. The lights in the houses were turned down and everyone was in bed. He looked down at little Jim. The funny old man's cap perched on top of a bunch of his dirty, unruly hair always made him smile. "I don't understand," he said, peering around in the dark. "What do you mean, Jim? I can't see anyone at all."

"They're all up 'ere, sir." In a flash, Jim was scrambling up a high stone wall and on to the roof of one of the shops. "Come up and see, sir!" he shouted, giving Barnardo a hand as he clambered up more slowly because of the awkwardness of his clothes.

As Barnardo climbed on to the top of the wall, the moon came out from behind the clouds. "It seemed," he said, "as if the hand of God had suddenly pulled aside a curtain."

Eleven children lay in huddled groups along the guttering of the roof. They had hardly any clothes on, and what clothes they had were torn in strips. Their faces were thin with hunger, and their arms and legs white with the cold, and yet they didn't stir as Barnardo and his guide stood looking at them. They were fast asleep; tired out with exhaustion, cold and misery.

"Come on, sir." Jim tugged at Barnardo's sleeve. "I'll show you some more. There's *lots* of 'em," he said, enthusiastically.

"No, Jim." Barnardo climbed slowly down the wall, and they walked on again, hand in hand. "I don't think I want to see any more. Let's go home."

5

A VISIT TO THE FISH MARKET

THERE was, so he told himself time and again, absolutely nothing he could do. But he was wrong. God had other ideas.

One night at a missionary conference in Islington, one of the main speakers was missing. As it happened, the Chairman knew Thomas Barnardo, and he also knew about Jim.

"On the spur of the moment," he announced, "I am going to call upon a young medical student from The London Hospital to describe the startling discoveries he has made about the children of the East End slums."

Barnardo was dumb-founded. But as always, once he had started talking, no one could help listening to him. The hall buzzed with astonishment and horror, and the speakers who followed might just as well have sat down and kept quiet. When the meeting ended, a young girl working as a maid shyly stopped Barnardo as he was leaving.

"I saved this for the missionaries," she explained, thrusting a small envelope into his hands.

"But you need it more." When he looked inside, he found twenty-seven farthings.

A week later, he received a letter. It was from the famous friend of the poor, Lord Shaftesbury. He was inviting Barnardo to have dinner with him and a few friends, so that they could learn more about the East End children. Now down to his last few pennies, Barnardo borrowed a suit from the house surgeon and walked all the way to Lord Shaftesbury's smart Mayfair house.

There were fourteen or fifteen people at dinner, and afterwards, Lord Shaftesbury challenged him.

"Can you show us these boys?" he asked, hardly able to believe the stories Barnardo had to tell.

"Any night you like, your Lordship," answered Barnardo firmly. "Come with me tonight after eleven-thirty and I'll show you."

They set out at midnight. The East End had never before seen such an array of finery clattering over the cobbles in a couple of hansom cabs. Drunken men tottering unsteadily home thought their eyes were playing tricks. Gentlemen wearing fine cloaks and hats and silk cravats accompanied ladies in coloured billowing dresses to the unlikely destination of Billingsgate Fish Market. There they gingerly alighted and followed Barnardo to the side-walks where vast tarpaulins covered the crates and barrels, keeping them dry and safe for the night.

"I'm not sure I believe you, young man," remarked Lord Shaftesbury, looking around. "I can't see a boy for miles."

"Not yet," replied Barnardo grimly. "But if you would just wait a moment." Systematically he began burrowing under the tarpaulins, feeling stealthily between the crates and inside empty boxes. Suddenly there was a squeal and a torrent of words.

"Lemme go! I ain't done nothin'! It wasn't me, sir, it wasn't, I swear it wasn't! Lemme go!"

Grasping an ankle firmly, Barnardo hauled out a frightened, spluttering boy, still half asleep.

"I'll give you sixpence to get the rest out," said Barnardo. And all of a sudden, the boy was awake.

He ran back, jumped up on top of the tarpaulin and started leaping and prancing up and down on top of it. Shrieking and grumbling, boys began crawling out, and more and more of them as Lord Shaftesbury began bouncing a few coins invitingly on the pavement in front of him.

Afterwards he took them to the coffee shop and bought food and coffee. There were seventy-three of them, and he felt as if somehow the whole affair must be a bad dream. As he watched them eating as if their lives depended on it, he said, "All London must hear of this."

And it was through Lord Shaftesbury, two years

after Barnardo first came to London, that Samuel Smith, a Member of Parliament, wrote a letter offering Barnardo a thousand pounds to continue working in the East End.

For ten days he kept the letter unanswered on his desk. He was going to be a doctor. He was going to be a missionary in China. He couldn't change his mind now.

But God, as Barnardo so often found, had other ideas. At last he replied to the letter—and he accepted its offer. China was very far away. Jim and his friends were right on the doorstep.

6

CARROTS

"LOOK out, Carrots! Your mother's coming."
The little boy queueing at the door of the pie shop stiffened. Instinctively his fingers closed tighter round the two precious pennies in his hand. He edged to the inside of an old man in front of him and stood there, trembling slightly, trying to hide his shock of grubby, bright red hair. Only three people in front of him, and then the steaming warmth and the smell of meat and fresh pastry. The thought of it made him feel weak all over.

"Get out of me way, you!" A stringy woman with a dirty apron and a cross disgruntled face elbowed her way through the queue. Her cheeks were flushed and her breath as she shouted smelled strong of alcohol.

"Get out of me way, you good for nothin's! Hiding me own son from me, his lovin' mother!"

Carrots wriggled his way in and out of the people and made a dive for the first doorway he came to. The door was shut and it wouldn't open.

He felt coarse hands and hard nails closing on his wrist, and he screamed dismally.

"Thief!" she cursed accusingly as she caught him, her hands forcing open his clenched fist and closing triumphantly on the two bright pennies. "I thought so!" She stood over him, shaking him, turning him upside down to see if any more money rattled out of the pockets of his tattered coat. "What I brought you into the world for, I don't know," she ranted on. "So lazy you can't earn more than twopence and so sneaky, you keep it all for yourself when your poor mother's faint and starving."

She tossed him down on the cobbles, looked around, and as Carrots scrambled up and ran for his life, she picked up a broom handle and gave him a solid whack which sent him head over heels on his way. Then mumbling and grumbling, she pocketed the twopence and hurried off to the nearest gin palace, still scowling.

Carrots lay in a corner and panted. Then he started to cry. He didn't often cry, but this time he just couldn't help it. He was so cold and so hungry. He had been overjoyed to find work that morning as a shoe-black. It was so cold that there were fewer boys than usual queueing for work so that in spite of his slight body and pale face, the man had taken him on for the day. And when it ended, he had forgotten all about the cold and the hunger pains in his stomach because he had twopence for himself, and he had run all the way to the pie shop, continually glancing back over his shoulder in case his mother was coming.

But it was always the same. The smell of food, the sight of it, and then—his mother. The shouting and screaming and kicking, and afterwards, the cold wind, nowhere to sleep, and scavenging endlessly for a crust or two of bread.

Carrots was eleven. He had been living on the streets since he was seven. He had never known his father and he wished with all his heart that he had never known his mother either.

He sat up slowly and rubbed his eyes dry with dirty hands. Then he saw a sight which made his hungry inside lurch with excitement. A young man in his mid-twenties was coming down the street, smartly dressed in a top hat and frock coat, with blue-tinted spectacles on his nose. Crowding round him were five ragged children, chattering happily, tugging at his hands, carrying his case for him; and he was looking down at them, smiling and laughing.

Carrots scrambled to his feet. If anyone could help him, Doctor Barnardo could. Carrots knew all about the big house in Stepney, which Thomas Barnardo had rented and cleaned and converted into dormitories for sixty boys. So far he had funds enough to provide for only twenty-five boys, but the news of what he was doing had spread like wildfire all over the East End.

"Please sir!"

Barnardo felt a slight jerk on his coat. He looked down.

"Please sir, please take me in, sir." Carrots was so faint he could hardly stand, and his wrists hurt where his mother had shaken him.

Barnardo tussled with himself. But he knew he could afford to provide for only five more boys.

"*Please* sir!" Carrots was on the verge of tears, but he didn't show it because they were all looking at him. "I'll do anything, sir, only please take me with you."

Barnardo had rarely seen a little boy who looked so stunted and miserable. "When did you last have a meal?" he asked, quietly.

Carrots shook his head. "Can't remember, sir. I 'ad a crust yesterday, but I ain't 'ad nothin' today, sir."

"I tell you what," Barnardo felt in his pocket and produced sixpence which he pressed into Carrots' hand. "You take that," he told him. "Buy some food with it, and as soon as I've a bed to spare, you shall come and live with us. I promise."

Carrots stared down at the sixpence. He didn't want it. He knew what was going to happen to it as soon as Barnardo's back was turned. He was tired and hungry and miserable and he felt like bursting into tears.

"Thank you, sir," he said. And turned away.

Barnardo, watching the thin, hunched figure walk dejectedly into the shadows, steeled himself and went his way. The decision had been agony, but there was no alternative. He would make a spare bed available as soon as possible; as soon as his funds could afford it. In the meantime, the one thing he would not do was to run into debt.

That night, Carrots' mother had a party in the Edinburgh Castle. She and her friends drank themselves silly on a fortune of eightpence. "It's not every night a woman comes by a bit o' luck," she told them, laughing.

Carrots spent the night walking, darting in and out of doorways, trying to evade the police. At last, down by the river by London Bridge, he found an empty sugar barrel and crawling into it, he curled up and went fast to sleep.

In the morning, it began to snow. Carrots half woke up, but he felt faint and dizzy, and so stiff with cold, tiredness and hunger that he drifted off into a kind of sleep again. A market porter found his body a few days later, still curled up in the barrel, and they said at the inquest that he had died from exhaustion, exposure and lack of food.

From that day onwards, every one of the sixty beds at the home in Stepney Causeway were always full.

"I'll never refuse a destitute child again," vowed Barnardo. "I don't care if I'm in debt or not. I don't care if I haven't a shilling in my pocket or a loaf in the larder. I'll never send another child away to die."

Then, in big capital letters that everyone could read, he had a large notice painted above the door of the house. It said: NO DESTITUTE CHILD IS EVER REFUSED ADMITTANCE.

7

TRAMPS, HORSES, AND A GIN PALACE

VISITING cards bearing the name of Doctor Barnardo began to appear in the most unlikely places. And one by one, the men who made their money in wicked ways began to feel a twinge of anxiety. It seemed as if nowhere were they safe from the Doctor's influence.

"Goin' in the fourpennies where the lords sleep, tonight, eh?" The Deputy in charge of the lodging house bantered with two tramps, a boy and a young man, as he took them up to the second floor dormitory.

"Fourpence each and out sharp in the morning," he muttered, dropping the money into a heavy, bulging pocket.

Barnardo hitched up the string holding his dirty pair of trousers several times too large for him, wrinkled up his nose, and turned to Mick, the boy with him. "I don't much like the smell," he remarked.

"Smell?" Mick sniffed loudly. "Can't smell nothin' meself. But you can't be partic'ler 'ere, Doctor."

Barnardo smiled and resigned himself. The oil lamps were so low that he could hardly see. Sitting on his bed so as not to attract too much attention, he felt in his carefully mud-stained coat for his spectacles and put them on.

The scene wasn't attractive. Over thirty boys were crowded into the long room, some of them lying on their beds smoking pipes, making the air more heavy and clouded than ever. The straw beds and iron bedsteads looked dirty and unfriendly.

"What about the lily-white sheets?" asked Barnardo wryly. Mick shrugged his shoulders. "What's wrong with 'em?" He picked up the corner of one of the stained calico sheets and inspected it. "Better'n most, sir." He stripped off his clothes, took everything including his boots into bed with him and shut his eyes. "Come on, Doc—'old yer nose and jump in," he advised, and promptly went fast to sleep.

Gingerly Barnardo took his advice and in spite of the smell of the yellow pillow and sheets, he was so tired that he went to sleep immediately. He was determined to know, once and for all, what his boys faced on the few occasions when they were able to afford a bed in a common lodging house.

Slowly and ingeniously his name was beginning to creep in and out of the dark places of East London. He seemed to have eyes that saw round corners and out of the back of his head; eyes that delved into the darkest corners of the dirtiest doorways, the most smelly back alleys. He could look at a bundle of dirty rags lying in a corridor and stop, instead of passing by, to retrieve a skinny, grubby, penniless urchin from beneath them. He could talk to the most defiantly independent children, well on the way to becoming skilled little street crooks, and persuade them to take a card with his name and address on it. And he knew that a few days later they would turn up sheepishly on the doorstep with a thumbed card held out, asking for a home.

One of the boys smoking a pipe in a bed farther down had put out his hand and taken one earlier when no one was looking. Before he left the lodging house, Barnardo was determined to give out a good many more.

But he never had the chance.

He had a nightmare. He dreamt that he had suddenly been found out. They all got out of bed and called him a spy, and then they began sticking pins into him and rubbing pepper in his eyes and nose and mouth. He seemed to burn and prick and sting all over. And then he fell out of bed and woke up.

The stinging and pricking sensation continued. His arms, legs and face were red and hot with irritation. He felt his face with his hands, and there were angry weals on his cheeks and down his neck. Then he looked at the bed. Scores of insects were running in and out of the sheets. Looking around in horror, he saw that the whole room was teeming with fleas and lice and bugs of every kind. Agitated, he pulled Mick out of bed, and the boy stood there, yawning and protesting, quite unworried by the army of night visitors, while Barnardo flung on his old coat and trousers. Then he grabbed Mick's hand and they ran past the astonished Deputy nodding sleepily by the door, out of the building and into the street and the fresh night air.

"What on earth's the matter, sir?" asked Mick in amazement. "Your face looks awfully funny," he added. It did. And Barnardo couldn't venture outside his front door for a week. But he had learned about lodging houses, and he was determined that as soon as he could, he would do something about them. He would open some lodging houses of his own.

But in the meantime, he remained undeterred and he was constantly on the look-out for new adventures.

Just before midnight, one day in June, he put on his topper and tails and called a cab. He was going to the Derby. It was a bit early to leave, said his friends, curiously, but Barnardo didn't agree. He wasn't going to see the horse-racing. He was going to find the forlorn straggling groups of street boys who made their way barefoot to the racecourse in the hopes of a field day picking the pockets of the rich.

The cab reached Epsom between three and four in the morning, and Barnardo made his way to the fish and chip stall. All around boys sat in little huddles, devouring a ha'porth of chips or gazing longingly at the stall, hands shoved deep into empty pockets.

Doctor Barnardo presented the astonished stall-keeper with as many halfpennies as he could find, and then he began to hand round packet after packet of fish and chips to the hungry children. They began to talk to him. Then they all sat down together on the damp grass, and he told them of his home in London and the boys who lived with him there.

At the end of Derby day, many of the children crammed into the cab as it rattled back to Stepney, where bowls of soup and beds with clean sheets were waiting for them.

But still the greatest challenge to the Doctor's work came from the great gaudy bars and gin palaces, full of loud music and bright lights, smoke and unhappiness.

When Barnardo realised that almost three-quarters of the boys who found their way on to the streets came from homes broken up as a direct result of drink, he vowed to take the public bars and the gin palaces by storm. With two friends, Joshua and Mary Poole, he took his stand outside one of the largest, the Edinburgh Castle. Jo played his fiddle, Mary talked about the Bible, and Barnardo himself distributed biblical leaflets.

The Edinburgh Castle was an imposing place. High and solid, built of brick, with pinnacles and turrets as grand as any real castle, the men and women inside forgot all about day and night, drinking themselves to a standstill listening to unpleasant stories and songs and looking at unpleasant pictures. Women who had their babies with them fed them on gin, and then roared with laughter when the babies went cross-eyed and the children couldn't stand up straight.

When they looked out of the doors to see what the music and shouting was outside, they ran to the upstairs windows and threw down pails of filth on Barnardo and his friends.

"The Word of the Lord," said Barnardo ruefully, "is not very effective when it comes from a mouth full of mud." So they started all over again and pitched a tent in front of the building. Fiddler Jo stood outside, and gradually people began to stop by the tent door to listen to the music. And then they went inside.

The tent could hold three thousand people. It was enormous, and at first everyone laughed at it. The owners of the Edinburgh Castle pointed at Barnardo's Bible House and roared with laughter. "He's mad," they said, "quite mad to think anyone will go to listen to the Bible when they can have drink and a concert hall for ten steps more."

But they were wrong. More and more people crowded into the sprawling tent. After every meeting thousands stayed behind. And of those thousands, hundreds pledged never to drink again. After a few months, four thousand people had left the gin palaces never to go back again. The great gaudy houses were more silent in the evenings, with only a few small groups of people half-heartedly watching the entertainment. And the owners began to scratch their heads in despair.

One day in October, a man called to see Barnardo. He looked seedy and extremely angry.

"I want to talk to you!" he began, blusteringly.

"Yes," said Barnardo politely.

"You know me, of course."

"I don't think I do."

"Oh yes you do." The man stamped up and down and banged his cane on the floor. "I'm the owner of the Edinburgh Castle. And because of you and your—your Bible thumping, I'm selling out. The least you can do is to buy the place yourself."

For a moment Barnardo was silent. He was stunned. It was the last proposition he had expected. It was quite out of the question—and yet the idea intrigued him.

"How much are you asking?"

"Four thousand pounds."

Barnardo's eyes didn't flicker. "Leave it with me. I'll think it over." He hadn't four thousand pence, but he could talk and pray and persuade, and he was determined to do all three.

But before he could do anything he read that the Edinburgh Castle was up for sale on the open market. There was to be an auction. Half an hour before the auction began, Barnardo made up his mind. He signed a legal undertaking to buy the Edinburgh Castle, and promised the money in a fortnight. Three-quarters of an hour before the fortnight ended, the last ten pounds came in. In no time at all, the builders and decorators had moved in.

The last thing Barnardo wanted to do was to demolish the old Edinburgh Castle altogether. He knew better than that. And he knew that everything could in some way be used to the glory of God. When the men raised their hatchets above the old bar where men and women and children had sat drinking until they collapsed, Barnardo stopped them.

"Leave it where it is," he said. "We'll do the same thing—we'll just do it differently."

Before long, the gin palace had become a coffee palace. Instead of lounging in the concert hall listening to rude songs, people listened to a different kind of music. Barnardo told them stories from the Bible, and men sat at clean marble-topped tables playing dominoes and drinking tea. Women learned how to make buttonholes from flowers, children joined the band and bashed drums, and men found that if they could manage to save a penny here and there in the Penny Savings Bank, the future looked a little less bleak. And at the old bar, re-painted, bright and shining, men and women queued for steaming mugs of coffee and tea, hissing out of the copper urns.

The storming of the Edinburgh Castle had been a great success.

8

THE DOCTOR TELLS A STORY

SOMETIMES people asked Doctor Barnardo to tell them stories about his children. And he held them spellbound. One day he told them about a boy called Punch who wanted to learn to read.

The story, he said, began in a thieves' kitchen in one of the narrow, dirty courts off Holborn. There was a common lodging house which had become famous because it was used as a hide-out by all kinds of criminals. Time and again the Doctor had tried to find a way to get inside the house, but the man in charge, whose name was Michael, never allowed him in. Until one day, at last, the chance came. It was midnight, and Michael came out to meet Barnardo.

"I've a sick feller in 'ere," he said gruffly. "I wish you'd see 'im, sir. I'm afraid 'e's got the fever."

Eagerly the Doctor climbed the stairs. "In one of the large sleeping rooms where fifty or sixty boys were lying on their beds," he said, "I found a fifteen-year-old lying ill in the corner with a sharp attack of rheumatic fever. When I told Michael that there was no danger of catching the fever and that I would willingly treat the boy and bring medicine free of charge, he accepted my offer."

He was inside the thieves' kitchen at last.

Soon he got talking to the boys and began to know them. They were all young—and they were all crooks. Their leader was a boy called Punch. Barnardo never met Punch because he was out later at night than anyone else, but when the boys talked about him, it was as if they would burst with pride.

Gradually Barnardo's patient began to improve. The fever died down, and the doctor was able to call later at night. His visits became regular occurrences, with all the boys sitting round the fire in the kitchen while he read a book aloud to them. And the later he came, the more boys joined his audience.

One night a boy he had never seen before caught his eye. He was crouching by the fire toasting a herring on the end of a long wire fork. He had bright eyes and a frank face. Instead of constantly glancing over his shoulder in the furtive way most young criminals did, he looked as if he hadn't a care on his conscience. "He must be new to all this," Barnardo thought to himself. And yet when the boy opened his mouth, Barnardo couldn't believe his ears. The words that came out were worse than those of all the other boys put together.

"Who is he?"

Barnardo's patient, wrapped up in a blanket beside him, opened his eyes wide in amazement. "Don't you know?" A look of pride passed over his face. "That's Punch."

From that moment, Barnardo made up his mind that somehow he was going to stop Punch growing up into a hardened criminal. But he knew that he would have to be very clever to do it.

He opened the book he had brought with him. It was *Uncle Tom's Cabin*, one of the boys' favourites. He was reading it for the second time over, and he realized that as he was reading, Punch was listening to every word, fascinated. At last it grew so late that he closed the book, and they all protested, as they always did, and begged him to go on.

"Who'd think," said Punch in amazement, "that there'd be such splendid stuff in a little bit of a book like that."

"That's the wonderful thing about books," Barnardo told him. "They're so small, and yet they hold whole worlds between their covers for anyone who wants to read them."

"You gotta learn to read first, though, 'aven't

you?" said Punch gloomily, staring at the fire. "I dunno more'n a street name or two and words over shop doors. 'Ow could I ever read a thing like that?"

Barnardo looked him straight in the eye. "You could soon learn if you put your mind to it."

Punch looked scornful. "Couldn't never spare the time, could I?"

"Why not?"

He burst out laughing—but it wasn't a very happy laugh. " 'Ow am I to live, I wants to know?" he challenged. "What'll become of my work?"

Barnardo took a deep breath. "That needn't be a difficulty. I can find you a home where you'll be given food and lodging free while you learn. That is if you want to go."

"Well I don't," said Punch flatly. Then he got up and went to bed.

After that, Barnardo always made sure that he came with his book under his arm late enough to find Punch in his usual position by the fire. And Punch never let him rest until he began reading.

"Couldn't you teach me to read when you come 'ere, sir?" he begged time and again. "At nights, when me work's done?"

"No." Barnardo shook his head firmly. He was determined to get Punch off the streets—and he was willing to wait until Punch was ready.

At last, one night, Punch stayed downstairs long

after the others. "I say, mister," he began, hesitantly. "How long d'you think it'd take to learn to read first rate?"

"If you put your mind to it half as thoroughly as you do to other things," said Barnardo, "you could learn to read in ten months or a year at the most."

Punch thought for a while. Then he glanced round to make sure they were alone. "I s'pose if I went to that there 'ome of yours," he whispered, "it'd be as bad as a reg'lar prison."

Barnardo threw back his head and roared with laughter. "What on earth gave you that idea?" he asked.

"I know those kind of places," said Punch darkly. "You can't do as you likes. They locks the doors on you and there y'are, stuck fast."

"If you say you'll come to my home for a year," promised Barnardo simply, "at the end of that year, you can go. If you say you'll come until you've learned to read well, then I'll let you go as soon as ever you can read."

A few nights later, Punch made up his mind. "Look 'ere, guv'nor," he said suddenly when they were alone, "I don't care what the others says. If you promise me honest that I can leave in a year's time, whether I've learned to read or not, then I'll go with you."

They shook hands on it. And in the days that followed while Punch settled in at Stepney, Barnardo learned from stray words here and there how he had learned to steal.

Punch couldn't remember his mother or his father. He had been brought up in the workhouse, and as soon as he was old enough and clever enough, he had run away to live on the streets. He ran errands, sold fuses, picking up a penny or two here and there. But he was only eleven, and the winters were cold. Days went by with nothing to eat and nights with nowhere to sleep, until at last he found a job near a railway station which brought him a treasure trove of a few pence. First he bought some food. Then he found lodgings and paid for a whole night's sleep in a bed.

He was in a large dormitory, and in the bed next to him lay a big, well-built boy, who seemed to have plenty of food and plenty of money. He sat on his bed telling stories of adventures that made Punch's eyes grow wider and wider.

In the morning, the smell of fog drifted up the wooden stairs. Punch put on his few rags, and went downstairs, hugging them dejectedly round him. It was starting to rain. Miserably he poked his nose round the door and wondered how on earth he could find a job. As he was standing there, the big boy came jauntily down the stairs behind him, whistling a tune and jingling some coppers in his pocket.

"Where you off to today?" he asked.

"Dunno," said Punch. "Ain't got nothin'. There ain't much doin' in this weather."

"Tain't bad weather at all—not for my game," said the big boy confidently. "Why not try it?"

"What d'you do then?" asked Punch in amazement.

"I do liftin'. I—prowl around, picking up what I can . . ." Putting his hand in his pocket, he brought out twopence and gave it to Punch. "If you falls on your feet, okay," he told him. "If not, I'll be near the pump at Aldgate this arternoon, and I'll put you in the way of earnin' yer livin' jolly quick."

Punch was right about the weather. And there was no work to be had. The twopence was soon gone, and he was soaked to the skin. In desperation he made his way to the pump, and before the afternoon ended, he had received his first lesson in stealing. In his hand he held a whole shilling.

"You prob'ly can't understand, sir," he told Barnardo. "One moment sir, I was starvin'. I 'ad nothin' in the world, nobody to 'elp me, no 'ome, no lodgin', nothing'. And then 'arf an hour later I 'ad a shillin' in my 'and. A whole shillin' to do what I liked with. And when it was gone, I 'ad only to get more in the same way. It seemed as if I'd come into a fortune."

It wasn't an easy life to forget. Punch settled down at the huge home in Stepney Causeway. He wanted to read, and he liked the Doctor. But he couldn't resist boasting of how good a thief he had been, and when the Doctor pretended not to believe him, he tried even harder to prove the truth of his stories.

"I say, sir," he said one day, "could you tell me the time, please?"

"Surely you can see the clock," replied Barnardo, testily.

"Yes I can, sir," persisted Punch. "But I want you to tell me the time by your watch."

Barnardo felt for his watch. Then he began to frown. His watch wasn't there. And neither were his keys. He went through all his pockets and they were empty. No purse, no handkerchief, no pencil or knife.

Punch, beside himself with glee, pointed to the writing desk, where he had neatly laid out everything he could find in the Doctor's pockets, without the Doctor himself feeling a thing.

It was only when another boy called him a thief during a quarrel one day, that the real horror of what he used to do came home to him.

"I thought 'e knew, sir," he said, on the verge

of tears. "I thought you'd told 'im. I never realized it before, but now I don't want to be a thief no more. 'E sounded like it were somethin' awful."

Punch learned to read in seven months. Barnardo gave him a Bible of his own, and a copy of *Uncle Tom's Cabin*, and at the end of the year, Punch asked if he could stay. He learned how to make boots, and then he began to teach other boys. "I get fifteen shillings a week and my grub!" he wrote triumphantly to Barnardo.

"Two years later," Barnardo told his fascinated audience, reluctantly bringing his story to an end, "I received an announcement. It was accompanied by a photograph of Punch and a lady whom I will call Mrs. Punch. No one could have recognized the good-looking, well-dressed young bridegroom in the picture, whose visiting card lay on my table, as the boy I had taken from the thieves' kitchen in Holborn.

"God be praised!"

9

ONE-LEGGED TAMMY

IT was winter and very cold. It was always cold in Edinburgh, especially in the slums, where Tammy lived in one room with his mother. He was twelve years old, and by working long shifts his mother was managing to pay for him to go to school a few hours each day. But this day was special.

They had twopence saved. Tammy grabbed it up and ran out to the pie shop. His split boots echoed on the icy cobblestones. If he hurried, he would be home again before his mother came in, and he could have the piping hot pie ready waiting for her.

It was getting dusk and the fog horns were sounding from Leith Wharf. Tammy's clothes were torn and the cold stung his arms and face, but he didn't really notice. He'd never known anything else. His father and his brother had died from fever when he was little, and as long as he could remember, his mother had worked until she was too exhausted to keep the two of them going. He ran faster, round the corner into the High Street, and streaked across the road, his eyes glued to the steam coming out of the warm pie shop, and the big notice fixed up outside the door.

"Watch out, laddie!" Tammy wasn't listening, as an old woman put out her hand to stop him. He hurtled across the road.

"Get out the way!" A covered wagon rattled full speed along the centre of the road, the horses' hooves thudding, their breath breaking through the fog.

"Careful!" One of the horses's hooves caught Tammy across the shoulder and he fell sprawling in the road. The next minute, the heavy wheels of the wagon rolled over him and thundered off into the fog.

Tammy vaguely heard voices shouting. Then he felt a horrible pain in his leg as someone tried to move him, and he lost consciousness.

The nurses and doctors at the Infirmary where Tammy woke up, were very kind. He had never before been surrounded by such comfort and love and attention. His leg hurt terribly, but the clean white sheets and the smiling faces made it almost worthwhile.

The doctor shook his head. He took a very long time examining the damage done to Tammy's leg, all crushed and broken from the heavy wooden cartwheel. Tammy's mother came too, and he saw with a shock that she looked older than he had ever seen her look before. Her face was white and drawn, and she didn't seem to know what to say to him.

"If you'll come with me for a moment," said the doctor, taking her by the arm and waving goodbye to Tammy, "I'd like to have a word with you."

He took her to his office at the end of a long, gloomy corridor. He motioned her to sit down, and when she didn't seem aware of him or of where she was, he took her arm again and led her gently to the chair.

"It's been a shock to you, hasn't it?" he asked, and she nodded. "But you know, it could have been worse," he went on. "Tammy could have been killed." Her eyes were looking away from his again, wandering round the small room, and he went on quickly, trying to hold her attention.

"I'm afraid, with your permission, we shall have to amputate Tammy's leg. It's so badly crushed that there's nothing I can do. And it's amazing," he added before she could speak, "it's amazing how well a youngster can adjust to getting around with a crutch. You wait and see."

There was silence.

"You do understand?" he asked her again, gently.

"What's that?" Her eyes hovered blankly back to his face again.

"You understand what I've been saying to you?"

"Oh yes." Her voice was as blank as her eyes.

"And I have your permission to operate?"

"Oh yes," she repeated flatly, and he led her to the door.

Tammy stayed at the hospital for many long months, lying flat on his back, gazing at the ceiling and wondering when he would be allowed to walk again. Eventually the day came, and his leg stump had healed so well that it hardly throbbed at all when he stood up, and he took a few hopping steps, holding the wooden crutch awkwardly, with the leather pad under his arm.

"You'll soon get the hang of it," the doctor told him cheerfully. Tammy nodded, But he wondered what kind of work he would be able to do with only one leg.

He soon found out.

People were not very kind or sympathetic when they met someone less clever or more clumsy than themselves, or in some way different, as poor Tammy was.

"We don't want cripples round here," they said at the factories. Tammy couldn't even run

errands, because all the other boys were quicker—
and most of them laughed at him.

His mother hardly ever said anything. She
looked sad and she cried a lot, and she seemed tired
out before she began her work. She grew thinner
and thinner, and then they laid her off shift
work because she was too exhausted to pull her
weight.

"We'll manage," Tammy told her, trying to
cheer her up. "God'll see to us. He doesn't
forget. He'll do something." But she just looked
away. It was she who had first told Tammy about
God and taught him to say his prayers, and yet
now, she seemed to have given up hope in
everything.

Tammy hopped off down the road and spent the
evening on the corner opposite the pie shop,
begging with his cap in his hand; and because he
had only one leg, quite a few people felt sorry and
stopped to talk to him and give him a farthing. It
was past midnight when he went home, and he fell
into his bed, his good leg aching after standing in
the cold all evening.

In the morning, he tried to wake his mother, but
she was dead. She had died from hard work,
exhaustion, and sheer unhappiness.

It took Tammy five months to walk to London.
He got a lift to Liverpool with a friend who

promised to help him, but when they arrived in the Merseyside city, his friend left him behind because it was too much bother to have a cripple in tow.

"Go to London," the boys said, as he talked to them in the streets. "There's enough of us here already. Get out and go to London."

So he began the long journey—because it is nearly 200 miles from Liverpool to London, and Tammy had to walk all the way. Sometimes the stage-coaches passed him, splashing mud up on to his tattered jacket, and he wished he could afford to ride with the rich people all the way to London. But he mostly avoided the big roads, because there were always so many horses on them, pulling coaches and carts and wagons, and he couldn't help remembering, and feeling frightened. Often, he slept under hedges and haystacks, and on very good days, when he made a penny or two begging or selling leather shoe-laces on the way, he spent the night between rough sheets in a lodging house.

He went on selling laces when he reached London. It was the only thing he could do because London, like Liverpool and Glasgow and Edinburgh, was full of boys trying to earn a living—only there were even more in London, and they were even sharper and dirtier and tougher, and just as they had done everywhere else, they laughed out loud at Tammy. That was what made Doctor Barnardo notice him.

It was at one of his parties for all the boys at a big lodging house. The feast had just begun, and before the boys at one of the long tables started eating, they all began jeering and shouting at Tammy.

"Hoots mon!" they giggled, mimicking Tammy's Scots accent.

"It's God-time now—bow your 'eads for grace, lads!" shouted one of them, pointing at Tammy and clapping his hands for silence. Another shut his eyes and folded his hands piously. "God loves little cripple boys," he said.

"And so he does," agreed the Doctor quietly. "And all little boys too, however badly they behave." A sudden silence came over the boys. They shifted uncomfortably, and for want of anything suitable to say or do, dived into the plates of buns piled on the table. After the meal, when Doctor Barnardo asked if any of the boys would like to stay behind and see about remaining with him in one of his homes, Tammy stayed behind, and they had a long talk.

Tammy hadn't a relation in the world. He had no money, and the last few nights he had spent out in the streets without anything to eat, getting colder and thinner and dirtier and more worried about the future. And yet for some extraordinary reason, he still clung obstinately to his belief in God. He still said his prayers each day however much the older boys laughed at him—perhaps because God seemed to him like the only friend he had to talk to. And now his obstinate faith had been rewarded.

He had found a home.

Doctor Barnardo didn't put him into a home especially for cripple children, because, unlike so many stupid people, he could see that Tammy had as much intelligence and fun and imagination as any healthy boy with two legs. Instead, he found him a job to do alongside boys who had nothing wrong with them. Tammy learned bootmaking from them, so that he could support himself, and while they worked, he told them all about Scotland, and the seagulls and the hills and the way people lived in the North, and they learned that a funny-sounding accent isn't something odd or frightening, but something interesting.

Best of all, in the Doctor's eyes, they learned to laugh *with* Tammy, and not *at* him, because when they got to know him, they found that although he only had one leg and a wooden crutch, he was just the same as they were.

10

FALLING IN LOVE

IT was one of those dark days in dockland. A grey mist hung over the East End, and steady rain beat on the blackened stone houses and trickled its miserable way down Stepney Causeway to the wharves.

Barnardo was twenty-six. He had been working in Stepney for five years, and in that time, he had changed. "Whenever he smiles," said one of his friends, "he beams benevolence. Kindness is written all over his face, and when he laughs, his laughter is infectious." While the rain teemed steadily down, he sat at his big desk writing. Then he heard a tap at the door.

A little girl stood outside on the step. Her name was Martha, and she was shivering. Her arms and legs were covered with cuts and bruises, and she was half-starved.

"Please," she said, gazing up at him, "do you take in little girls?"

Barnardo took in Martha. Standing there looking down at her, there was nothing else he could do.

As soon as possible, he found her a home with some friends of his, because it was impossible to have a little girl living in a big house with hundreds of boys. But for a long time after that, he kept wondering how many more Marthas there were in London—and what he could do about them.

★   ★   ★

In the meantime, he received an invitation to a party. It was a party for poor boys to be given in Richmond by a young lady called Syrie Elmslie.

There were cakes and buns and tea to drink, and the ragged children ate as much as they could cram into their mouths. Then they listened with bated breath while the Doctor laughed and joked and told vivid tales from the Bible.

"Don't go!" they begged him when the party came to an end.

"I wish you didn't have to go, Doctor Barnardo," agreed Syrie. But dusk was falling, and his boys would be waiting for him at home. Reluctantly he tore himself away.

The next day he had business to attend to in the West country. "Paddington station, please," he told the cabman, and they rattled off across the cobbles.

Barnardo had a sheaf of papers with him to study in the train. He had photographs of all his boys, taken when they first came to him and then again when they had been with him for a while. Gradually he was building up big files of case histories, giving the names, the ages—where ages were known—and the background of all the children, until his information was like a grand social survey. Hurriedly he jumped down from the cab, paid the driver, and enquired about his train.

As he reached the platform a voice behind him said "Why, Doctor Barnardo! What a coincidence to meet you again so soon!"

He turned around and found himself face to face with Syrie Elmslie. "Please—" she began, turning to her father for approval, "please do join us on our journey."

Her father, smart and rich in his silk top hat, frock coat and high top boots, nodded genially. "By all means, by all means. Join us, do," he said. "It'll be nice for Syrie to have someone to talk to—I generally nod off. The movement, you know," he added. "The movement—most soothing."

When no one was looking Barnardo felt anxiously in his pocket. Luckily there was a little extra money there for emergencies.

"I wonder if you would excuse me for a moment, Ma'am," he asked Syrie, and hurried away to pay the extra amount so that he could travel in the First Class compartment.

Then for the next few hours, they sat and talked. Mr. Elmslie, as he had promised, dropped off to sleep almost before the train had pulled out of Paddington, but Thomas Barnardo and Syrie Elmslie hardly stopped talking.

"Do you know," said Barnardo, "I think we both dream the same dreams and share the same longings. How interesting and exciting it is to talk to someone who thinks as you do." And Syrie was captivated by the unusual, lovable young man, whose heart was bigger than all the rest of him put together.

"Thank goodness I came to my senses in time," she thought to herself, remembering the days not so long ago when she had tossed her head through endless parties and dances and social occasions, spending a fortune of her father's money, until a friend had pulled her up by remarking frankly, "Syrie—you're a little heathen!" Thank goodness she had listened to him and made up her mind to change her ways. Thank goodness she had found work to do which had led her to meet this extraordinary, adventurous, amusing young man, sitting opposite her in the railway carriage, talking so enthusiastically about his plans.

Suddenly the journey was over. Mr. Elmslie had to be woken up and they said goodbye to Barnardo. He shook his head as he went slowly on his way.

They had talked so much, about so many things. And yet he had said nothing at all of the one thought uppermost in his heart. He wondered whether there was anything Syrie also had left unsaid.

They didn't meet again for eighteen months. Barnardo was shy, and he had his work to do. It was absorbing work, and there was always more of it than he could cope with. It would have been lovely to share it all with someone—but he pushed the idea to the back of his mind. Syrie was so kind and so thoughtful, and she was very attractive. He was plain and so poor. She seemed a thousand miles away from him, and her home at Richmond was very far removed from the rowdy, romping home at Stepney.

But when they suddenly came face to face at a funeral all those months later, Barnardo couldn't hide his happiness. He was overjoyed to see Syrie again. And she seemed delighted to see him too.

"In that railway carriage," he said, stumbling a little with shyness and excitement, "in that railway carriage, there were so many things I would like to have said. But I hadn't the courage . . ."

Syrie smiled. "There were things I wanted to say, too," she said. "I'm so glad we've met again."

One month later, on the 17th of June, six thousand people crammed into the Metropolitan

Tabernacle in the heart of the East End of London to attend the wedding. Everybody came, from the rich friends and relations in their silks and satins, their toppers and tails, to the poorest of the East End poor. There was shouting and singing and tears of joy, and Barnardo's boys leaped up on to the ends of the pews to form an archway for the bride and groom to pass under.

They set up home in Ilford, Essex. Always hard up, always finding it hard to make ends meet, Barnardo revelled in the love and security of a home of his own and the hope of a family. But even when their first child—a little boy—was born, he still couldn't forget that dark day in Stepney and the little girl called Martha. A regimented home like the one for boys in Stepney wouldn't be right for little girls. But what he wondered, was the alternative?

One night he sat, bolt upright, in bed.

"I've got it!" he shouted, waking Syrie in his excitement.

"I know what we're going to do!" he told her, overjoyed with the scheme, although he hadn't the faintest idea where the money or the land would come from. Then he began to describe to her a little village with family cottages, a school and a church and a village hall with a weathervane. In each cottage there would be a "mother", and a family of girls ranging in age from babies to teenagers.

And because he was Doctor Barnardo, and once he had made up his mind nothing could deter him, he found suitable land within a short walk from their home, and he raised the money to build on it. Soon fourteen cottages were standing round the green, and the Barnardo's attended the opening of their Village Home for Girls.

11

THE DOCTOR TELLS ANOTHER STORY

"ONCE upon a time," said Barnardo, "I was standing in Gin Sing's Concert Room very late at night. There were sailors dancing, fiddling and drinking. A few moments after I arrived, I saw something peering quietly round the door . . ."

It was a small figure covered with a shawl. And when the shawl parted slightly, Barnardo could see two large grey eyes and a wise, solemn face. But it belonged to a very little girl. She glanced questioningly at the barmaid, who shook her head. Then she slipped out of the door again as quietly as she had come in.

"What on earth can her mother be thinking of to allow her to come to a place like this so late at night!" Barnardo exclaimed.

The barmaid shrugged her shoulders. "Nobody lets her. She's her own mistress—she does what she likes." she said. "She's here most nights, looking for a job."

"Looking for a *job*?" Barnardo wondered if he

had heard correctly. "Whatever does she do, and who does she do it for, at this time of night?"

"You'd hardly believe what that girl can do," the barmaid told him. "She can scrub a floor as well as anyone. One of the girls often gives her a job." She nodded towards a group of street girls laughing loudly in the corner. "But they often keeps the little 'un waiting half an hour."

"Who is she?"

The barmaid propped herself against the counter. "Her name's Rose. About ten years old, I'd think—she's a brother a year or two younger'n herself. They lives in one room in Rosemary Lane. The girl promised her mother to look after the boy when she died, so she does the cleaning and mending by day and then works at night to get the money for the rent and enough to send the boy to the Ragged School. She'd do anything to keep 'em off the streets, that little 'un would," she said.

Barnardo had heard enough. He thanked the barmaid and hurried outside. The little girl was still there, as he hoped she would be, waiting in the shadows, her shawl pulled up round her face, watching the door for a sign of an employer.

"You've had to wait a long time," Barnardo said sympathetically. "You must be tired."

He never forgot her reaction.

"The child eyed me icily from head to foot," he

said, "pulled her ragged shawl closer round her face, and deliberately turning her back on me, slowly sauntered away."

He only made things worse by following her and calling out, "Don't hurry away—I only want to help you." The footsteps quickened, and in a few moments, the little girl was out of sight.

Guessing she was going home, Barnardo cut through the back alleys and arrived at Rosemary Lane first. He was just in time to see her disappear into one of the most notorious houses in the neighbourhood, full of unpleasant people.

"I saw and felt instinctively," he said, "with that intuition which comes from long experience as a fisherman in the muddy tide of the London streets, that my fish was very shy, and that no ordinary bait would suffice to win her confidence."

The only bait he could think of was a woman worker in the East End. He went and told her the story, and she called at the home in Rosemary Lane and persuaded the little girl and her brother to come and have tea with her. Then she invited Barnardo to join them.

When he arrived, Rose took one look at him, stood up, pulled her brother up with her, and said she wanted to go home. It took a great deal of talking and tea and buns to persuade her that there was no trap, but only an honest offer to help.

When the two children got up to go she invited the Doctor to come to tea at Rosemary Lane the following day.

Barnardo went home deep in thought. Rose was very independent. She had worked terribly hard, but she and her brother had a room of their own and she kept it spotlessly clean and tidy. He knew it was going to take all his quick-thinking and persuasion to make Rose give up her freedom.

The next day was Saturday. When afternoon came, he set out to keep his appointment.

Rose and her brother lived on the top floor of the tall house. Barnardo climbed up the battered staircase as far as he could go and found the front and back attics occupied by different tenants. The corridor between the two had been boarded in with plywood with a rough door hung in it. Inside, with no windows, the door opening on to the staircase, lived the two children. The butt end of a candle flickered dimly in a corner, and as Barnardo pushed open the door, he found Rose on her knees with her dress tucked into her apron, scrubbing the floor.

She didn't stop scrubbing. Instead she half turned and nodded briefly. "How do you do?" she said. And that was all.

Barnardo stood and looked around for a bit. All the time the energetic scrub, scrub, scrub went on.

"Rose, I suppose you know what kind of people live in this house?" he asked at last.

She nodded.

"And I suppose you know that most of them are very wicked?"

She nodded again, and went on scrubbing in silence.

"Have you never thought that perhaps if you live long enough among wicked people, you may one day become like them?"

This time there was more reaction. Rose tossed her head and glanced up at him scornfully. "I can take care of myself!" she said.

"I know," said Barnardo, playing his trump card. "But what about your brother, Patsy? What would happen if you fell ill and weren't able to take care of him?"

He knew it was his trump card, but he had no idea that it would produce such a violent response. Rose hesitated and stopped her scrubbing. Her face went very pale, and then her cheeks began to flush scarlet.

"Supposing you were run over in the street or caught a fever," he went on quickly. "You wouldn't be able to look after Patsy as you do now, and then what would happen to him? You know the kind of boys who live here—young thieves and pickpockets . . ."

Rose scrambled up off her knees. "Oh stop, sir, please stop!" she sobbed, leaning against the wall. "Please go away. I can't bear no more. Go away!"

Barnardo left. And when he had gone, Rose sat down and thought. She thought of the times she had been forced to fight with the boys in the house to rescue Patsy from them. And she thought of the lost, lonely feeling she had known when their mother died. If anything happened to her, Patsy would feel like that—and he would be completely alone.

The next time Barnardo called, Rose didn't ignore him. She made tea, and then she said, "I've been thinking about what you said, sir—what you said about a home for Patsy and me . . ."

"One hardly expects to find heroes and heroines disguised in the rags of street children," Barnardo said to his listeners as he finished his story. "But what is heroism? The dictionary defines it as 'the quality of a hero: bravery, courage, intrepidity.' The heart of a hero may beat beneath the rags of a street waif as well as in the breast of a warrior whom the world worships.

"That is why," he said, "I call this story The Story of a Little Street Heroine."

12

THE SHILLING BABY

"THERE now! Ain't she a beauty?"

Doctor Barnardo looked—and he felt like bursting into tears.

The woman had come swaying into his afternoon surgery, when he sat in his office interviewing people who wanted to come and live in his homes. Her breath smelled of alcohol, and her clothes were gaudy and stained. She had a bundle clutched in her arm under her shawl, and as she spoke, she opened the shawl and deposited the bundle on the table in front of the Doctor.

"Well?" she demanded, when he didn't answer her immediately. "What you got to say? Ain't she bonny?"

She stood with her hands on her hips, breathing heavily and still swaying slightly, waiting for some kind of response.

But Doctor Barnardo couldn't take his eyes off the baby. It must have been about two years old, but its arms were no thicker than his fingers and its face looked worn and serious and sad, like the face of a very old man, all grey and wizened. There was silence while everyone waited for the Doctor to say something. The baby didn't cry or gurgle like most babies do, it just sat where it had been dumped, with a few ragged pieces of cotton tied round it, and looked lengthily round the room with its solemn, tired eyes. When it had finished considering, it took hold of a lump of some kind of food tied up in rags and attached to its waist with string, put it into its mouth, and sucked it for a while.

"Well," said the woman impatiently. "D'you want her or don't you?"

It was quite true: Doctor Barnardo did want the baby. He had heard about her from a fellow worker who lived near the woman's lodgings. The baby didn't seem to belong to anyone. It was the common property of the household, although the woman who had brought her to the Doctor seemed to be more in charge of her than any of the other women in the house. The baby spent all day crawling round the courtyard alone, in and out of the doorway, wearing the same filthy rags week after week.

"How old is she?" asked the Doctor, wearily picking up his pen.

"About two years old, she'll be," said the woman, all of a sudden very eager to please. "Two years old and a little lovely." She pushed the child playfully on its bottom in a gesture which was meant to look full of love.

"Is she ill?"

"Well now, you can see for yourself," she said indignantly, gesturing towards the forlorn little bundle on the table. "She's the bonniest in the city. Lor' knows I'll miss her."

Her smile, meant to be encouraging and flirtatious, was more like an ugly grimace, and the Doctor hurried the interview to an end. He had seldom seen such an unpleasant woman, and he couldn't wait to be rid of her.

"Very well." He wrote the child's name and age on a piece of paper. "You needn't wait. Leave the child here and our Matron will come over and pick her up and take her to our Village Home for Girls."

There was a short silence. Then the woman leaned towards him. Smiling, and putting on her softest, silkiest voice, she said "What are you going to give me for her?"

"I don't understand." The Doctor put down his pen and looked up at the woman. "The child isn't even yours. She's a bother to you, and I am offering to relieve you of that bother, to take the child and look after her and bring her up properly. I would have thought *you* should be owing *me* something."

"Well I ain't." The woman thumped her fist down on the table, and the baby continued to sit gazing mournfully around. "She's worth half a quid to me, and she don't go for no less."

Barnardo was Irish, and he had his fair share of temper. He had no intention of paying for the child, and he said so. Ten shillings—fifty pence—was a great deal of money, and if he paid for one baby, he would have all the women in the East End of London on his doorstep wanting him to buy their babies. Much as it hurt him to see the child and the state it was in, his conscience wouldn't allow him to give in and do something as wrong as paying for a person.

"Very well then!" The woman glared at him, whipped the child up off the table, wrapped her shawl round her and stormed off out. "You'll never get her till I has the money!" she shouted back at him.

"Quick!" Barnardo called one of the men working with him. "Follow her. See where she goes and what she does. We've got to have that child somehow."

As he might well have guessed, the man followed her to the nearest public house. She sat the child on the bar, where it continued to sit and contemplate as if it was still in the Doctor's office.

"You can't earn a decent penny from no one,"

she started off loudly to the barman as he poured her a gin. "They'd leave children to die in the gutter rather than pay an honest woman an honest penny . . ." Bit by bit, loudly and very distorted, with a great show of tears and affection, the story was told.

"More fool you," said one of the women in astonishment. "He'll have you in gaol before you knows where you are. I'd go back quick if I was you. He might still take her."

An hour and two gins later, she was back.

"There y'are, guv'nor. You shall have her for a crown." Barnardo clenched his fists. He was gaining ground. But he was determined to stick to his principles. "No," he said sternly. "I shall not give you five shillings. The child isn't yours. You have no right to her. You haven't even looked after her properly. Leave her with me, and I will do all I can. But I will not give you five shillings."

The woman sniffed, rocked about a bit and shed a few tears. "Well," she said, thinking hard, "half-a-crown."

"No."

She muttered and sobbed to herself for a while, and then, at last, with a reluctant shrug, she said "Well, guv'nor, let's be friends. You shall have her for a bob."

The Doctor faced his new "friend" across the

table. He looked at her and felt quite overcome with her extreme unpleasantness. Then he looked at the baby, already so harmed and unhappy and spoiled by all the nastiness that had surrounded it. He couldn't bear to think of the child growing up like its guardian.

"I shouldn't," he sighed. "But for the child's sake, I will." He rang the bell on his desk and handed the woman a shilling.

"Ta guv'nor," she said, hurrying off. "Ta guv'nor. Cheerio then."

The Matron of the Infirmary where the Doctor held his surgery took the baby to the Matron of the Village Girls Home. Neither of them had ever seen such a sad, filthy little bundle of rags before. Even the girls working in the cottages stopped their cleaning and tried to do something to help as they began, as gently as they could, to clean the child.

But it was a puzzle to know how to begin.

There *was* no beginning. There were no pins or buttons or hooks or eyes. There were just rags, knotted together with string, and they hadn't been taken off for weeks. In the end, the only answer to the puzzle was a pair of scissors, and the rags fell away.

Underneath, the two-year old child was like a little skeleton, and the lump attached to her waist, wrapped up in a dirty cotton rag, which she had sucked and munched at for three weeks or so, was just an old fish bone.

*   *   *

A year later, Doctor Barnardo was invited to tea at Peablossom Cottage, one of the little red brick cottages in the circle that made up the Village Home for Girls. A group of girls lived in each cottage, with a "mother" to look after them. Their ages varied, and the oldest helped to keep house and look after the babies, just as they would have done if they had been part of a real family. As often as he could, the Doctor visited the different families, and heard the latest news of all his children.

It was a long time since he had been to Peablossom Cottage, and it was a very special occasion. They sat him at the head of the table, and put the petted baby of the family beside him, and by the end of the tea, she had completely won his heart. She had curly hair and chubby cheeks, and she looked so happy and mischievous that he couldn't take his eyes off her.

He scratched his head and turned aside to whisper to the cottage mother.

"I can't understand it," he said, bewildered. "I thought I knew all my girls, but I can't place your baby. She's such a pet. Who *is* she?"

"Don't you remember?" she replied, smiling and looking from the Doctor to the little girl sitting proudly beside him in her best bright dress. "You should. She's the Shilling Baby!"

13

BUT there was one story he loved to tell more than any others. It was a story that Jesus told.

One day a man gave a big party and invited all his friends to come to it. When everything was ready, he sent his servant out to call them. And they all began to make excuses. One had bought a plot of land and he wanted to go and look at it. Another had bought five pairs of oxen. It was rather like buying a new car—he wanted to make sure he hadn't been cheated. Another was newly married. "I can't come just now," he said.

So the servant returned and repeated all their excuses to his master. They sounded very silly, and his master was angry.

"Go out again," he told his servant. "Go into every street in the city. Search in the courtyards and the back alleys, and bring in the poor and the lame and the blind to share the feast with us." And the servant went out and found hundreds of people who never had a square meal or any kind of fun, and he brought them all back with him and there was still some room left.

"Go out again," said the master. "Go and look in the fields, and on the park benches and in the dark ditches, and make them all come in to fill my house."

So they came and they ate and drank and sang and shouted and laughed because they had never seen such a feast before. The master and his servant were very happy.

And outside, the men who had turned down the invitation looked in at the lights and the excitement. They peered through the cracks in the bolted and barred windows, and they wished that they had gone to the party after all.

When the Doctor held his Waifs' Supper every New Year, it was just like that.

There were poor children in their rags and tatters clamouring to come in. There were the sad, the dirty and the neglected; the crippled beggar children, hopping in on wooden crutches. Sometimes there were boys who had walked so far that their bare feet were cut and bleeding, but they hardly seemed to notice because they were so delighted to be allowed in.

Two thousand boys came, crowding into the gaily lit Edinburgh Castle. There were plates piled high with cakes and buns, and big mugs of hot tea.

A band played music to welcome them in, and when every scrap of food was eaten, there was a magician to watch, music to listen to, and a troupe of dancing dogs.

Tired feet and a dismal future were quite forgotten in the fun, and by the end of the evening, the Doctor had hundreds of new boys queueing up to be given a place in one of his homes. He beamed on them in delight, chuckled with them, scolded them and comforted them. And perhaps they, in their turn, helped him a little when he lost first one of his own children, and then another, from diphtheria. But he still had Queenie and Marjorie, Cyril and Stuart and Frederick, to frown and smile upon, as close to them as any other father to his children, in spite of his enormous "other family".

Before he was fifty years old, Doctor Barnardo had rescued more than twelve thousand children from the streets. He called them his children. "You are all God's gifts," he told them. "God has given you to me." Sometimes he stopped working and went to his window to watch them playing in the courtyard below. If they were laughing, it made him laugh too. But if they were quarrelling or crying, he hurried down and wanted to know why.

Before long he was circulating meal tickets to magistrates, telling them to give one to any hungry child and send him straight to the Edinburgh Castle for a hot meal of meat and carrots and dumplings; and when he discovered a man, imprisoned for keeping his children away from school because he couldn't afford to buy them boots, he began to circulate boot vouchers too. Because it was sometimes difficult to find jobs for his boys when they left the homes, he began a scheme enabling them to emigrate to Canada where plenty of work was waiting for them, and in London, he opened two lodging houses for children only, and a hospital with eighty beds in it next to his home in Stepney Causeway. When a member of the hospital staff was about to arrange the fitting of a legless girl with artificial limbs, he said it was to be done "as carefully as if she were my own daughter", and later, it was the proudest moment of his life, when the Chief Surgeon from his old training school, the London Hospital, came to see his handicapped children, and was so astonished at the imagination and skill with which they had been treated that he exclaimed, "Oh, give me a few minutes to think! I never saw such a sight as this. Everything has been done for them that surgery can do."

He delighted in thinking up new ways of helping his children. And he felt sure, as he watched them growing strong and happy, able to make friends and do a job of work and enjoy doing it, that God delighted in them too. Because the Doctor was still very close to God. When he was worried about a boy, or at his wit's end to know where the next penny was coming from, he went off on his own and talked it over with God. And somehow, things worked out.

"Strange as it may seem," said a friend of his, "he believes in God as a kind of telephone exchange of the universe, who graciously allows himself to be rung up whenever any of his creatures need anything to carry on his work.

"Doctor Barnardo prays, and the Divine Manager at the Central Celestial switches on Barnardo to any number of subscribers, who hear the cry as a voice from God, and send money in accordingly.

"Fantastic, is it not? Quite mad! of course. But the cash comes in . . ."

Soon he had opened more homes—homes for handicapped children, nursery homes for babies, holiday homes by the sea and hostels for boys at work. And when his children left, he never lost touch with them.

In one month, he received over 27,000 letters and dictated as many replies.

"I enclose two stamped envelopes so that you may write to me whenever you like," he would say.

"Each envelope is marked 'Private', so that none will open it but myself; if you have any little secrets to tell me, they will meet my eye only." And in return he received gifts from the poor and the young which delighted him: a pound note from a North Country farmer as a thanks-offering for the safe delivery of his lambs; sixpence from a child who gave up sweets for a week; fourpence from another who earned it catching mice.

He was never idle for a moment. Before he was sixty, he had suffered two heart attacks, and yet when he recovered, he seemed as enthusiastic and energetic as ever. He dictated letters, caught cabs, and travelled in trains; chivvied his patrons and harassed his staff, and worked so late that he usually went fast to sleep on the way home. One day however, in the early evening, he felt very, very tired.

"My head is so heavy," he said to Syrie. "Let me rest it against your face." He was thoroughly tired out, and he quickly fell into a deep sleep, from which he never awoke.

There had never been so many people thronging the pavements of the East End of London as there were to see the Doctor's coffin taken to Liverpool Street on its way to the Village Home where it was to be buried. Thousands lined the streets. Tenement houses where the poor lived were draped in black, and flags flew at half mast from all the public houses. The boys' band played, women cried, and even the men couldn't trust themselves to speak without a lump coming into their throats.

It was like losing a friend.

14

TODAY

TODAY, more than a hundred years since Doctor Barnardo opened his first East End school for ragged children, there are over six thousand children in the care of Barnardo Homes. There are Homes throughout the world for both sick and healthy children, black and white, rich and poor. Few of them are orphans, because today there is less poverty and less disease. But there are other reasons why children need to be cared for.

Joanna's mother brought her on a cold January day. She had on a thin, dirty cotton dress, a pair of sandals and no socks. "This is Joanna," said her mother. "And I'll be glad to get rid of her."

Helen arrived with a typewritten guarantee: "Helen appears to be a normal baby in good general health." Jill's mother told her she was taking her to a home for naughty girls because she was tired of looking after her. Michael is spastic, and frightened of going to visit his mother because she is angry when he knocks things over. Matthew is three years old. He has dark skin and bright blue eyes and he loves wearing yellow clothes. His parents are not in touch with each other, and his mother is so backward that he already finds it hard not to be impatient with her.

At Christmas time, the mother of Barbara and Jennifer telephoned to ask what presents they would like, but when Christmas came, she forgot to send a card. Carol is half-caste. For the first few weeks at school, she was always in tears. "They keep calling me nigger," she confessed at last. "And I don't like it."

What is it like to be part of a Barnardo family today? It isn't always easy. But it is usually easier than what has gone before. Marion runs away again to find her mother and she is sent to a remand home for stealing. Margaret and Diana are moved to another home to be nearer their mother and step-father. And there is a feeling: the feeling when someone branches out and leaves a family. An unsettling. A moment of unsteadiness and wondering—because this isn't home and these aren't parents, and Margaret and Diana are already part of another family.

But gradually it is back to normal. Carol coming in to show off a new sweater; Jill asking if she may introduce her first boyfriend; Jennifer talking endlessly about carrying the Girls' Brigade Standard at the parade on Sunday; six-year-old

Helen writing to Headquarters for a baby to join the home, and helping to dress and undress a protesting Matthew.

And so the family lives together. Week by week they face the ups and downs that all families know —and the problems that most families don't even dream of. The girls will go on to hostels in the big cities, to offices and shops and factories. For boys like Matthew and Michael it may be harder, because Matthew is half-caste and he is intelligent; and people who don't know Michael laugh at him because he can't speak very clearly.

But at the moment, the house is quiet. Jill and Joanna and Barbara are at the youth club in the church across the road. Jennifer and Carol are at Red Cross. And Helen is telling Matthew a story.

"If Jesus was here," she says, "he'd sit you on his knee and tell you all about the Little Green Engine without looking at the book . . ."

But Matthew is already asleep.